Tiger Runs

By Derek Hall

Illustrations by John Butler

Sierra Club / Alfred A. Knopf

San Francisco   New York

Tiger is feeling so bored. Her mother has gone hunting for food. Hunting is very dangerous, so Tiger must stay in a safe place.

Tiger wants to play.
What's that? Something
is moving in the grass.
She trots over to see.
It's a beautiful butterfly.

Tiger tries to touch the
butterfly, but it darts away.
She scampers after it.
Again and again she tries
to catch it with her paw.

Tiger is lost! She has chased the butterfly for such a long way. And now it is raining. She sits down and cries like a kitten.

Suddenly, there's a noise!
Tiger looks up, frightened.
A huge elephant is lumbering
towards her. It's the biggest
animal she has ever seen.

Tiger turns and runs, faster than she has ever run before. She is running like the wind, and crying for her mother.

Tiger hears her mother's roar, and runs to meet her. Tiger's mother is very cross. But Tiger is so pleased to see her again.

Tiger's mother soon forgives her. They lie down, and Tiger climbs on to her. She purrs happily, feeling safe once more.